7 STEPS TO

A SALE

By

BW GATES

Table of Contents

Introduction   3-10

Chapter 1 Attitude   11-14

Chapter 2 Why people buy   15-19

Chapter 3 Urgency   20-22

Chapter 4 Seven steps to a sale   23-25

Chapter 5 (1) First Moments   26-30

Chapter 6 (2) Agent & Company Credibility 31-34

Chapter 7 (3) Discovery   35-45

Chapter 8 (4) Information Confirmation & Ownership Commitment   46-48

Chapter 9 (5) Product Demonstration   49-53

Chapter 10 (6) Objections   54-59

Chapter 11 (7) Closing   60-67

Chapter 12 General topics   68-75

Chapter 13 Stories that sell   76-85

Chapter 14 Conclusion   86-89

Before beginning this book on how to increase sales production I want to make one thing very clear.

Identifying **PAIN** or **GAIN** underlying emotional motivation is the primary focus for all successful selling. That is the methodology and thinking premise behind every word in this book. Everything you are looking for and all follow up questions deal with generating some emotion. This will only come from something specific in the potential customer's lives. Good or bad experience is not the issue.

A certain emotional state must be present before a sale can be made. Facts and figures. Features and benefits are never enough. Having a sensitivity to their unique personal situation is necessary. This process can be consistently duplicated. Always know where you are going and what you are looking for.

FADIPOC is a living, breathing entity that changes with every new potential customer or client. Getting them to share something personal with you is what opens the door for mutual communication. Only then will they better listen to how you can help them.

Find an emotional chord to attach your message to. Your "message" will always be to buy your product or service right now.

INTRODUCTION

- **WIFM**. What's in it for me? This is the underlying stimulation that creates desire. Everyone has unique personal self-interests pulling upon their current actions and thoughts.

- Every topic of conversation should be to awaken emotions. Always looking for **PAIN** or **GAIN** subject matter.

- People buy new things because they are excited and stimulated.

- **DBM**. Dominant buying motive. This is specifically why they will buy right now.

- Uncover primary emotional reason for taking action immediately.

- Only two compelling directions. **PAIN** or **GAIN**! Either they want to remove a current problem or take a step forward to improve their life or company's situation? That is, it! Find it.

- The entire sales process is to first find that special something. Then satisfy it.

- Hopefully they will have both forces pulling upon them. Every topic of conversation should be directed towards these two areas.

- Which has the most powerful influence?

- Once you do uncover some personal bit of information that is important to them. Stay on just that topic. Get them fired up. "Tell me more".

- **Carefully listen and skillfully question** upon question to bring that experience back to life.

- It is the third or fourth follow up question on an emotional topic that will uncover the golden nuggets of true motivation.

- Get them thinking and talking about anything that excites them.

THREE MENTAL STATES

In two out of three they will not buy.

- **Open**. Receptive. The only place where they will buy. You have managed to actively involve them in the process of improving their current situation. They must be talking and participating to be open.

- **Processing**. Confused or distracted. Must go home to think about it. Gave them too much information or they still have other options to explore. Will not buy now.

- **Closed**. Negative. Not listening and will never buy anything from you. Short answers, no eye contact, arms folded and silent. All bad things for your cause. Your questions are not opening them up.

- During a presentation customers will often move from one state to another.

Give them time to process your solution. Their active participation is crucial in moving them towards open.

BODY LANGUAGE

- Arms folded, legs crossed or no eye contact. Not engaged. Bad.

- Leaning forward, responding to questions and involved. Good.

- Non-verbal signals are huge when determining the customer's current state. Be sensitive to their every move and mannerism.

THREE TYPES OF PEOPLE

- **Visual**. Use charts, graphs and video presentations. These people rely upon their eyes. Show them what they want to see.

- **Auditory**. Sound is powerful. Get them to talk. Ask directed questions that let them hear the benefits from their own mouths.

- Why would you want more bedrooms? Where would you put the new TV?

- What would you use the extra space for? Why would you need all this memory for your computer?

- Be quiet and let them hear their own answers.

- **Tactile/Kinesthetic**. Touchy, feely people. Get them involved "hands on" with your product. You can hug them.

FOUR COMMUNICATION STYLES

- **Analytical**. Seek order and details. No small talk. Data only. You still must get them emotional but do it quickly and with short sentences.

- **Driver**. They want to be in charge. Give them choices. Don't waste time. Encourage them to lead you to where they want to go.

- **Amiable**. Decisions based upon feelings. Make a friend. Be slow and methodical.

They will buy into you as a human being as much as your product or service.

- **Expressive**. Risk taker. Decisions based upon opinions, hunches and intuition. They enjoy talking about themselves. Encourage it to happen.

- Adapt each presentation to the unique person in front of you. You want to project an image of energy and certainty without running too far out in front of them.

  - Communicate in ways most comfortable for them not you.

  - Everyone has a pace. Slow or fast. Mirror theirs. Match their mannerisms.

  - Be sensitive to how they best receive and process new information.

SUMMARY

- Overall goal is to find a primary emotional buying influence. You do this with great questions

- Be sensitive to their situation and personality. **PAIN** or **GAIN** is always where to look.

- Move buyer's emotional state from closed or processing to open and receptive. They must be engaged to buy.

- Be aware of all non-verbal body language signals.

- Determine which type of person. Adjust presentation to them.

- Communicate on their terms.

Chapter 1 **ATTITUDE**

- Always be positive and upbeat.

- Leave problems at home when going to work.

- A smile goes a long way towards a better connection with every customer.

- People can feel your attitude and energy. Give them something positive to embrace.

- Only 10% of all thought and mental power comes from the **conscious brain**.

  - That part of the brain only determines yes or no responses using past data. Tends to dwell on negatives and encourages inaction. It takes five positive thoughts to erase one negative.

  - Being too analytical will cripple the emotional flow of a sales presentation. You must program your brain (and your customer's) to minimize the conscious brain's influence.

- Always maintain an optimistic attitude. See things as half full not as half empty.

- 90% of all thought comes from the **subconscious brain**. This hidden force is much more powerful and influences all thoughts and actions.

  - Subconscious mind does not distinguish the difference between the truth and a lie. Right or wrong. Has no moral judgment. It just wants to create and bring to life whatever is currently being fed in.

  - Sole function is to summon what you are currently thinking into becoming reality. It is a huge powerful source of energy and capable of most anything.

    - Constantly deliver positive thoughts and visions to yourself.

    - Anything is possible. You must faithfully believe, and you will ultimately achieve.

- You are responsible for your destiny. No one else.

- Write down goals. View them often. Hold yourself accountable to realistic numbers.

- Seeing them every day will make them more obtainable.

- Be specific about number of calls necessary, sales presentations to make and exact amount of money to be earned.

- Practice sales presentations with friends, family and co-workers. Much less expensive way to learn and improve.

- Every salesperson is an actor on stage. Each sales presentation is a new performance.

- Preparation breeds confidence.

- Have a set direction for every presentation. (Follow the steps to a sale). You are always looking for something important on their mind that will get them engaged.

- Emotion, excitement, and energy bring out the checkbook to buy.

- It is never just facts and figures or features and benefits. The proper emotional state that encourages a new purchase can come from any topic.

- It can be past or present, positive, or negative in their lives. Encourage and inflame emotions about anything. Get them to feel something.

  - Get them stirred up and then tie your product or service to their current emotional experience.

  - Stimulate their brain and awaken their heart.

Chapter 2 **WHY PEOPLE BUY**

- Use active listening to uncover emotional reasons for action. Always looking for **PAIN** and **GAIN** topics.

- Focus on not only what is currently being said. More importantly on what is implied and how they are feeling at that very moment.

  - Be sensitive to their internal voice. Is it worth the pain of giving up my money to obtain this benefit?

  - This is what they are thinking. Must create value specific to them.

  - **Ask** why are they considering making a change in their lives right now?

  - If you did buy; why would you? What do you hope to gain?

  - Why do business with me? What can I deliver to you now that you don't already have?

- Get any response to that question. Even imaginary or unrealistic.

- People buy somewhere between their wants and needs. Get them to respond and share with you anything about their business or personal situation.

- Emotional satisfaction is the most powerful motivator.

- Have them describe in great details what they seek. When? Get their timeframe.

  - Best question ever: **Why is that important to you?**

- Emotion and enthusiasm not logic close most sales.

- Don't complicate the sales situation. Offer less choices and things to think about.

  - Be selective and repetitive. Allow them to talk about specific things they want. Only address these issues.

- The customer should speak at least 60% of the time.

- Practice being silent. Salespeople talk too much. You can't be the one that is always talking.

- Early questions must be good enough to get the customer engaged. Once you get them going on any emotional topic. Just get out of the way and encourage them to dig deeper into themselves.

- They will feel from within to see the benefits outwardly that they are seeking.

- Pull every ounce of energy out of any personal insights they are sharing. **"Tell me more"** should be used often. Why do you say that? They must be the ones talking. Not you!

- A **feature** is only a physical characteristic of a product or service.

- A **benefit** describes how that feature will emotionally satisfy a customer's wants, needs and desires.

  - People buy benefits, not features. Uncover the most desired needs and wants. Discuss just a few select features that can deliver those benefits for them.

- **USP**. Unique selling proposition. What makes your offering stand apart from all the others? You must have answers and stories for that concern.

- Never negatively sell against or bad mouth your competitors. It is always bad form and will reflect poorly upon you.

- Know what your product can offer that the others cannot.

- Product knowledge is a fine line to walk. Don't share too much. Stay only on topics they have mentioned and are interested in.

- Motivations to avoid loss or failure are often stronger than feelings towards achievement and upward mobility.

  - Current ownership problems are where to look for this. Bring them painfully into the light. Help them to feel their unhappy situation.

- Dissatisfaction drives people to seek new and better solutions.

- "If you could only change just one thing about your current product or service; what would that be?"

- Allow the customer to awaken their own unique emotional situation.

- Have patience and let them speak. They will show you how to sell them if you can slow yourself down and allow it to happen.

- Use well directed questions to help them uncover and awaken their emotional passion for change.

  - Keep digging for more. Second, third or fourth questions about a single emotional topic or concern will eventually bear fruit.

Chapter 3 **URGENCY**

- Urgency is more of an attitude and energy level rather than a specific combination of words or actions.

- Walk fast. Talk fast. Be excited.

- Always move with a strong sense of purpose. Being energetic is contagious. So is a bright smile.

  - Propel them forward with your own momentum and enthusiasm.

  - Have a "get things done" atmosphere surrounding all your actions and words.

- Create the fear of missing a special "today only" offer or opportunity. What they want may be gone tomorrow.

- Use the innate greed factor in most everyone.

- Fear of losing out on a once in a lifetime incredible opportunity is often more powerful than the unfocused desire for something new.

- Excitement moves immediate needs and wants ahead of procrastination. A heightened emotional state is essential.

- People always want a great deal. You must determine what they perceive that to be and then give it to them.

- Encourage emotional clarity about specific customer wants and needs. Allow them to put themselves into a new updated personal ownership vision.

- To do that they must be speaking. Not you.

  - The more that they talk about what they want the easier and more clearly, they can see it happening right now.

  - Have them describe your product as already being in their lives. How would they feel? Bring a beautiful current ownership experience alive and into the present.

- Reasons for purchase must be specific. Combine that vision with a "one time only" special deal that cannot be refused.

- On a scale of 1 to 10 how important is improving your life today? What will make this a 10?

- By numbering their priorities, they become more real and immediate for them.

- Create specific value, special circumstance, and atmosphere of opportunity. Use their words to personalize today only benefits.

- Time and immediate solution become more important than delay to achieve what they want.

- Have massive amounts of positive energy to share with others.

- Urgency is created from the very first moment you meet someone. Move and talk with purpose, conviction and direction.

- You are there to solve a specific problem. Bring the situation to full light and leave no doubt that it can be fixed right now.

Chapter 4 SEVEN STEPS TO A SALE

- Know where you are going during every sales presentation.

- The people will be different each opportunity, but you always know what you are looking for. Emotion!

  - Have a repeatable pathway. A logical sequence.

  - Each sales step to be completed. None skipped or omitted.

  - Trust that each of the 7 steps brings you closer to your goal of satisfying their want or need. That gets you paid.

- Visualize each sales step as a box to be checked off in your brain. Think and see in your mind's eye the acronym **FADIPOC**. "Fhad eee pock". Hear the sound and see each step.

  - **F**irst moments.

  - **A**gent and company credibility.

  - **D**iscovery.

- Information confirmation.

- Product demonstration.

- Objections.

- Closing.

- Keep it simple and stay on track.

- Emotion and customer involvement need to be present.

- Know all the steps to a sale forward and backwards. The order may change during a presentation but they all must be accomplished.

- You can ask them to buy at any time. The more times the better.

  - Trial closes get them used to hearing the words "buy now".

  - **Never start selling in earnest until after sales step number five.** You create value and genuine desire for a specific item before you can discuss dollars.

- You start every presentation by making a friend and earning their trust.

  - Discovery uncovers their reason for action.

  - Product demonstration clarifies the exact solution.

  - Objection handling and closing skills makes it easier for them to say yes.

  - Stay on path. Along the way continually keep them emotionally charged up.

Chapter 5 (**Step 1**) **FIRST MOMENTS**

- Be professional. Smile often. Be genuine. Only one chance to make good first impression.

  - People only buy from people they like and respect.

  - Be a friend first. Credible consultant second.

  - Absolutely no selling.

  - Get the customer to talk about themselves.

- Get personal. Find something to like about them.

  - Kids, rings, hats, clothes, speech accents, shoes, jewelry, etc.

  - Liking them first will help them to like you. It really works.

  - Pretend you are at a party and just met them. Make a new friend.

- Encourage them to share something about themselves.

- Ask open ended engaging questions that the customer will enjoy answering.

  - What is your story? Please tell me about that ring, tattoo, hat, etc.

  - How old are your kids? What are their names? Talk to everyone. Get everyone participating.

- Make direct eye contact. Use their names often. Include all children.

  - Did I pronounce your name correctly?

  - Recognize that women are major decision makers most often in sales situations. Get them involved early.

- **Order of the day** or **Intent statement**. You are there to solve their situation right now.

  - Tell customer in a soft way that you are going to ask them to buy. Much less threatening when done early.

- "You will have the opportunity to make a choice here today. Please keep an open mind. Is that fair?"

- Get verbal confirmation to proceed. They must acknowledge what you have just said.

- Don't try to slide over any uncomfortable situations or awkward moments. They won't just magically go away.

- Be strong and purposeful in what you are doing. You are there to help them.

- Keep the dialogue open. If they resist anything you say, ask them why they are feeling that way?

- **Breaking the pact** up front. (Couples often tend to agree not to buy anything just before going out shopping). In their minds they are just going out to look.

  - Bring it up. Don't be afraid to talk about it.

- Say something to the effect of: "Most people before leaving the house make an agreement between themselves to never buy anything that day.

- No matter how good the deal or how badly they need change. Did you two discuss that?" Wait for their answer.

- "That is perfectly normal". Laugh with them. Keep it light. Just do me a favor, if you see a better opportunity than what you currently have now, will you at least give it serious consideration?

- (yes) Have them say it out loud.

- This verbal confirmation gives them permission to buy later.

  - If you don't remove this hurdle up front, then they will make liars out of themselves if they do buy later.

- Allow them to get comfortable with you. Just like meeting anyone new. Best way to make a new friend is to talk about things they are interested in.

- That will always be about them and not you.

- It is so important that they see you not as a threat or just another salesperson trying to make a buck.

- Trying to sell or qualify them before they accept you as a person is a tough hurdle to overcome later.

- Have patience and never rush into your discovery section too soon. They should be comfortable enough to share with you before you earn the right to probe into their desires and concerns.

Chapter 6 (**Step 2**) AGENT & COMPANY CREDIBILITY

- **USP**. Unique selling proposition. As mentioned earlier, you need one. Yours should be the very best option available right now for their particular situation.

  - Have specific and compelling reasons for doing business with you and your company.

    - Why should they act right now?

    - Why should they buy your product and not something else?

    - You should have really good answers in your own mind to those two important questions.

  - Discuss with the sales manager or other associates how to address these issues. It depends upon what you are selling.

- People buy people as much as they buy products and services. Be different. Compassionate and special. Great listener.

- Be someone people want to do business with.

- Dress well and act polite. Speak clearly and always act with deliberate purpose.

- Softly tell the customer what the product won't do.

  - Credibility comes from always being honest. Dropping little mini negatives about your product will keep your presentation more real.

  - Always do exactly what you say you are going to do.

  - **Be on time.**

  - Never guess or bluff an answer. If you don't know an answer to any question or concern, then go find it.

    - Once you are caught in a lie or give an incorrect answer then you are done!

    - To make any point don't just tell it. Instead ask it as a question. Let them answer. Their voice is much more powerful and credible than yours will ever be.

- If you made this product yourself, would it have that feature? (yes) You just answered your own question.

- What are some of the things you look for when doing business with a company? (We have that)

- What have you heard about our company? Have you owned our product before?

- Uncover any past negative or positive impressions. Know their complete history and all past ownership experiences.

- Have previous customer testimonials.

  - Display personal, company and industry awards. Trophies, plaques, and special photos speak louder than your words.

  - (Let them see them without you commenting).

- Be organized, professional and personable.

Chapter 7 (**Step 3**) **DISCOVERY**

- Most important step in entire sales process!

  - If you don't find out the "why" then they are never going to buy.

  - Take as much time as necessary. They speak more than you do. Get them engaged.

  - Get them talking about something personal in their lives. Anything!

  - This is the point where you are looking for third level involvement. I will discuss that soon.

  - Stimulate their brain cells.

- What emotional priority has the most influence upon them right now?

  - **DBM**. Dominant buying motivation. They do have one. Find it.

  - Listen for and direct all conversations towards subject matter that deals with their personal current situation and desired lifestyle.

- Work, family, hobbies or previous ownership experiences are always good places to look.

- Stay focused on wants and needs. Probe and stimulate to determine and heighten just how much they want them.

- **PAIN or GAIN**? You will see those two words over and over here. Some stimulation must be present in order to offer a solution.

  - **PAIN** Obtain relief from perceived negative influence or situation. Painful past regrets that they will not repeat.

  - **GAIN** Burning desire for improvement. Upward mobility. More prestige. Desire for a new and wonderful improvement to their lives.

  - Help them see a positive step forward they can now obtain.

- The more detail and elaboration the better.

- Don't get ahead of yourself and stop listening. Thinking about what you are going to say next may cause you to miss their one key element of motivation.

  - Listen to their words and feel their passion. You can't do that without giving them your full attention.

- Customers will help you to sell them if only you will let them.

- Recognize **3 LEVELS** of **EMOTION**

  - **Level 1** is just statement of **fact**. My dog is brown. No real involvement in what is being said.

  - The "dog" can be anything important to them.

  - **Level 2** is all the **memories** and **experiences** associated with the dog. Special moments recalled. Painful or joyful are both good. The juices begin to flow.

- **Level 3** is the huge, massive swirl of **emotions** surrounding the entire dog ownership experience. This is where you help them to go. Uncover any emotional connections to specific life events that ignite passion.

- Find them and stay on them.

  - It is your careful questioning and listening skills put to the test.

  - Find any level 3 events. All level 3 emotions generate positive and very necessary brain activity.

  - Tie your product or service to those specific emotional chords of energy.

- Don't just uncover facts (level 1). You want emotional reasons for action (level 3).

- Identify current priorities of primary user.

  - On a scale of 1 to 10 where does this potential purchase lie? Why?

- What are some 8's and 9's in your life? How can this be a 10 for you and your family?

- If money was not a factor and you did buy it right now, why would you?

- Some primary motivational factors include timing, price (value) and immediate solution.

- Family. Job. Hobbies. **What has changed?** Why now?

- Eliminate alternative solutions. Your product or service needs to receive budget priority.

  - Why did you decide to buy this? Go into detail with them. Know their thought process. Play devil's advocate if necessary.

  - They need to feel comfortable enough with you to share their personal visions and desires.

- Depending upon your specific product or service, what is your competition?

- Why do they see your product as their best solution? Ask them. Don't assume.

- What, when, and why do they want it? Are there any current problems being experienced?

  - Concentrate on asking better, more personalized open-ended questions.

    - Get them to talk. Eliminate yes or no answers.

  - Follow the emotional path. Once a personal priority is revealed.

  - Each subsequent question is used to raise their involvement and energy level.

  - Your next great question is always related to their last answer

- "**GAIN**" questioning. What do they see as being better for them?

  - What does get you excited?

  - What has changed in your life?

- Job promotion. Marriage. New child.

- If you did have the money, why would you buy today?

- Why have you always wanted one of these?

- How would owning this improve your life? Please tell me how you see that happening right now.

- Why don't you own one already? Why buy today?

- Something good happen at work? Birthday? Anniversary?

- **"PAIN"** questioning. Find current discontent. Uncover emotional and economic cost of current ownership.

  - What do you own now? How long have you had it? What do you like most about it? If you could only change one thing about it what would that be?

- Put an actual dollar value on their pain. How much are you spending now? Go into great detail.

- Help them to feel the money currently being spent in as many ways as possible.

- Write down every single expense. Let them see and feel it.

  - The more stirred up you can get them emotionally the better.

- What will the new one do for you that you are not getting now?

- What has been your worst ownership experience? How did that make you feel?

- Why are you considering a change?

- Are you missing work to be here now? Time is important to everyone.

- Do you enjoy shopping all over town?

- **"Tell me more"** is a great response to anything they say.

- After a negative reply to any closing question: "But if you were going to buy today, why would you do it?"

- Often the very reason they give for not buying is exactly why they should!

  - Dig into every answer looking for passion.

- Don't be put off by any negative responses. Store them away and look for new directions.

- Get used to hearing "no" without being discouraged.

- Getting someone to spend money takes time. Have the patience and confidence to believe you truly can help them.

- **"Why do you feel that way"** can be asked all the time in most any situation.

- It is never one specific question that matters or opens the information door. It is what you do with the answers that are important.

- Find emotional passion using question upon question. Peel back the emotional onion layers of motivation.

- Follow up questions are the essential key to uncovering genuine passion.

- It will never be the first or second question that produces emotion. It will be the third or fourth.

- Speak softly to emphasize an important point. People will listen more intently.

- Changing voice inflections keeps your presentation more vibrant.

- Discovery time is spent learning the important information necessary in order to be able to ask them to buy later.

  - Keep everyone in the present tense.

  - Any references to doing something at a future date must be challenged.

  - Genuine emotion will always move the timetable for action forward.

- Make their situation important enough that it can only be solved here and right now.

Chapter 8 **(Step 4) INFORMATION CONFIRMATION & OWNERSHIP COMMITMENT**

- Most overlooked step in the entire sales process.

- Confirm and verify what was learned during Discovery.

- Rephrase their PAIN and GAIN. Make it real and pressing.

- Get confirmation that you heard and understand their situation. Earn the right to solve it.

  - **This is the very important transitional step between listening and selling**.

- Restating their needs, wants and pain clarifies why they should buy today.

- They must say out loud that your solution is an improvement to their lives. Get **verbal** confirmation that your offering can solve their current situation.

- An ownership commitment must be emotional and very specific for them.

- Paint them into a mental "ideal scenario" of dream ownership. They must see themselves already in possession of your product or service.

- Forget about money! Right now, I just want to hear you say that you want it and see it as a better way to go.

  - Where are you going to put this new thing?

  - Who is going to use it first? Where?

  - Both their mouth and mind must be receptive to new ownership. As they speak, they will better see and feel possession.

- Do you agree that owning this would be positive for you and your family? Why? Tell me more.

  - Would you own this today if you could?

- We are not talking money now. We are talking about improving your life. Do you agree that this would do that?

- **You must get a commitment to own (at some point in time) or you will never close the sale**.

  - Are you determined to improve your current situation? Why?

  - How different would your life be if you owned this now? Tell me more.

  - Do you truly feel that you want and deserve this? Why?

- Get an ownership commitment from everyone involved. Every person involved should speak. Even the kids.

  - Get them excited. Have them explain out loud why they want it.

Chapter 9 (**Step 5**) PRODUCT DEMONSTRATION

- Don't show off your product knowledge. Too much information will cause customer overload and confusion.

- You want them "open" not in "processing" mental mode.

- Only talk about features important to the customer. Just what was uncovered during Discovery and that is significant for them.

- Better to discuss just one single important benefit five different ways than to introduce five different things all at once.

- Safety and reliability are always good topics.

- People don't buy features. They buy the benefits associated with them.

- Introduce a single feature then have them describe the benefit they see coming with it.

- Their voice is much more persuasive than yours. The more customer participation, the more interest and excitement generated.

- Paint usage and enjoyment experiences with the most visual words possible. The customer must see themselves owning and using your product.

- Identifying unique benefits exclusive only to your specific product are powerful messages.

- Create value and opportunity in the customer's mind. The better the mental and emotional pictures they can visualize, the more sales made.

- Emotional excitement generates the energy necessary to produce behavioral change.

- If they are not charged up, then they will not act in a timely manner.

- The more they touch and visualize ownership the more they will want it.

- Product demonstration creates value in the customer's mind. They must see themselves owning and using whatever you sell.

- Have them tell you how they see their new future after the purchase.

- Give just one effective product presentation on a single specific product selected just for them.

- Be focused on something in stock ready to be delivered.

- Who will be using it and how? Get them to touch it.

- Don't talk too much. Silence is your friend and very powerful.

- Give them time to absorb what their hands and eyes are experiencing.

- Let them attach their priorities and concerns to the solution you are offering.

- Allow them to mentally see your product in their home without hearing your voice distracting them.

- Get them emotionally and physically involved.

- Ask trial closing questions all during the demonstration. Is this what you want? Do you see the benefit? Please tell me what you are thinking? How will this help you?

- Let them touch and experience for themselves. Don't do simple tasks for them unless they ask for help.

- Never discuss price during the product demonstration. Must first build sufficient value and stimulate desire.

- Sell benefits standing on your feet. Only talk money while in your seat.

- Be mostly silent but always helpful when necessary. Let them experiment and learn for themselves.

- Give them time to create their personal ownership pictures. They must first play with your product, or they will never pay for it.

- Have them list all their "must have" features. Create a scenario where they must give up one thing.

- Which one can you live without? Why that one? Go into great details to determine their ultimate priorities.

- This process promotes an air of concession. Your product or service does not have to be perfect and probably never will be.

- It just must satisfy their most pressing emotional want or need at this moment.

- Using the scale of 1 to 10 is the easiest way to prioritize their desires. Make a list of all the must haves.

Chapter 10 (**Step 6**) **OBJECTIONS**

- Welcome objections. They are a sign of interest. They are your friends.

  - See objections as opportunities to do business.

  - Only fight one battle at a time. Don't get involved with multiple problems all at once.

  - There are no such things as objections; just "concerns".

  - Don't interrupt. Let them express their entire list of why no action today.

    - Only then you can address them one by one.

- Recognize difference between a condition and true objection.

  - Often a stated condition is the very reason why they should buy.

- A condition is only a pause or excuse. A small matter that must go away before action can occur.

- An objection is a stop sign. A specific reason why someone will not take any action immediately.

- Sufficient customer emotion, passion and involvement will remove most objections.

- Real objections are repeated. Acknowledge and ignore first time heard. Just move past it.

  - If you hear it again then isolate and overcome the second time around.

    - Once solved then verify they are satisfied with your solution. They must speak.

- Uncover real reasons behind their concerns. Restate what you think they mean. Confirm this with customer.

  - Constantly remind them of the things they want to accomplish.

- Have this solution be more important than anything they might be giving up.

- Get a firm commitment to move forward if the concern can be resolved.

  - Use every objection as a closing opportunity.

  - So, this is the only thing keeping you from taking this home right now?

    - If I can get that done for you then you will be our newest owner today?

- **Objection sequence**

  - Empathy (not sympathy or agreement). I can appreciate how you could feel that way.

  - Restate in softer terms whatever the concern. Isolate this as the final issue before purchase.

- Question their resolve. What do you feel are the benefits of doing it that way?

- Get history and background. Have you done it that way before?

- Establish their ideal timetable for accomplishment. If things went perfectly; then when would you want to close?

- Impact statement regarding delay. Be very specific about their costs in dollars, time, and continued pain. Pause! Let them speak next.

- Paint a clear vision of their new and better life once owning your product or service.

- Solution. Let's not talk about what we can't do. Let's figure out what we can do to get this done right now.

- **Higher authority** situation (attorney, accountant, family members, etc.).

- Let's practice what you are going to say to them. Let them hear their own words describing perceived benefits.

- If you could buy it right now, why would you?

- **Feel, felt, and found**.

  - Feel is the acknowledgement (not agreement) with whatever objection is raised.

  - Felt is the switch or transfer of focus.

  - Found is the solution or proper direction.

    - I understand exactly why you could **feel** that way. Many of my clients had **felt** the very same way. But after owning the product for just a short time. They **found** they are saving more money and living more fulfilled lives.

- **Isolate**. Is there anything other than money that would stop you from owning today?

  - On a scale of 1 to 10 where does this lie? Are there any 10's?

- No matter the stated objection. Always go back to **PAIN** or **GAIN** motivation. Emotion and excitement will melt most objections away.

  - Reiterate what they have already said. Further elaborate the current problem or potential reward again and again.

  - Help them to clearly see a desired solution they can receive right now.

Chapter 11 (**Step 7**) **CLOSING**

- Successful closing is all about positive attitude. It is the end game towards you getting paid.

  - Act like you have been there and done that before.

  - Never let a customer see you sweat. Be prepared to walk away from every deal. Stay strong and purposeful.

  - Be on the same team with them even when exerting pressure to act immediately. No pressure. No sale!

- After asking a closing question always remain very quiet!

  - **Let the silence build**. He who speaks next often loses. Let them figure out how they are going to pay for it.

  - You need to be more persistent at asking them to buy than they are stubborn at resisting your efforts to sell.

- Find several ways for asking everyone to buy today no matter what they may say.

- Ask them to buy at least 5 different times.

- Closing is a collective marathon of effort and persuasion. Not a quick one-time short sprint.

- Always get a verbal ownership commitment before talking specific numbers.

- You can't close on something they don't want.

  - Big mistake is going into the economic weeds before they have even said that they want to own it.

  - Have them say out loud that they do desire the perceived benefits.

- Don't be weak at this crucial point in time.

- Give a choice within a closing question with either answer being good.

- Do you prefer paying with a check or credit card? Do you want the red one or the blue one today?

- Use trial closes all during the sales presentation. The earlier non-threatening agreements you can get upfront then the easier the final close will be.

  - Does this make sense to you?

  - Is this important to you? Why?

  - Can you see yourself using this right away? Please tell me more.

  - Do you want this color? Why?

- **Don't talk through the close**.

- When the customer says "yes" you stop talking and start filling out paperwork. No more selling.

- Don't risk adding in some new variable or concern with more information.

- **Apology close**. Put blame on yourself for their inaction.

  - I must have done or said something wrong? You have convinced me that this product is everything you want and need. It must be me.

    - What have I done?

- **Ben Franklin close**. Make a big "T" at the top of a blank sheet of paper.

  - Left side are the reasons for buying right now. Right side are the reasons for not acting.

  - You help them prepare all the reasons for doing it right now on the left. Make a long list.

- Slide paper and pen over to them to prepare their reasons against. Don't challenge or say a word. Stay silent. Let them think.

- Build Ben up to add more credibility to this method. This is how he made all his important decisions.

- He was first self-made millionaire in America. His decisive actions made America great.

- If it is good enough for Ben, then it will be good for them as well.

- Obtain a minor point of agreement to get the major purchase commitment.

  - If I do add the extra battery, can we wrap this up right now?

  - Would you like delivery included at no extra charge?

- Today you get a choice. You can either continue what you have already been doing. Or start a new chapter in your life.

- Which sounds better to you?

- **Assumptive close**. Have paperwork ready.

  - Who has the best handwriting? Let's get the paperwork started.

    - Just slide the papers over and be quiet.

- Closing phrases. (Put them into your own words).

  - All figures aside, is this the model you would like to own?

  - What is your most important consideration for making this decision today?

  - Is there anything else you can think of that would make this deal perfect for you?

- What are some of the key benefits for you to own this right now?

- Aside from money, anything else stopping you from becoming our newest owners today.

- What is the worst thing that can happen to you if you do buy it?

- Ask plenty of trial closing questions all during sales presentation. They are a way of taking the customer's temperature.

  - You are looking for the best value, right? Do these numbers seem realistic to you?

  - Do you see the benefits of owning this top-quality product for a longer period of years?

    - The warranty will protect you from all those expenses you have been facing lately.

  - Do you agree this will satisfy your needs?

- Do you feel this makes more sense than what you are currently doing?

- Always save a valuable piece of information or free bonus for the second or third closing attempt. **Don't give everything away too soon.**

- People need to say no a few times before they feel good about saying yes.

That is, it! Those are the seven steps you should always cover during every sales presentation. You should be familiar with this specific pathway. Find ways most comfortable for you to get through them all. Every question and topic of conversation is searching for emotion from **PAIN** or **GAIN** subject matter. They must talk and be involved in the entire process. Along the way you are internally checking off each of the **FADIPOC** boxes.

Chapter 12 **GENERAL TOPICS**

Economics and value only matter after the emotional commitment to own has already been made. Don't talk money too soon.

Use customer questions as the basis for asking yours. Why is that important to you? If it did have 40 megawatts of power or 26 cubic feet of storage, would you buy it right now?

Get the customer involved in clarifying exactly what they want. Have them tell you out loud why they want it.

More cash upfront means a higher probability of closing the deal. "Up to" is good phrase to get more money for increasing either initial cash down or monthly payment.

Stay broad range and not specific money amounts early in the negotiations. Keep them more flexible.

People will agree to much higher dollar amounts than they are willing to admit if they are excited and badly want your product.

Proper paperwork upfront will make all deals easier to close later. Get complete customer information early. Write everything down accurately. Use proper spelling and full names. These are legal contracts.

Ask for referrals. They are essential for any lasting sales career. "Of all the people you know, who is most likely to be in need of a new product in the near future?"

Why did you pick them? Get more information. A warm lead is much better than just a name and phone number.

Let's call them right now to set an appointment. I will treat them with the same respect and integrity that I have given to you.

Keep customers involved. Stop often during your presentation to ask: What do you think of that?

Can you see yourself using it? How? Tell me more. Why is this good for your family? Help them to see the benefits.

Allow them the time to visualize ownership.

Don't waste time discussing features and benefits that have no value to the customer. Too much information is always bad.

Be specific with them. Only talk about the 3 most important things they want. Don't bombard them with all 20 miracle things that your product can do.

Say the same one important thing 5 different ways instead of introducing 5 different features.

Building value is showing enough positive difference between what they are doing now and what they will soon be getting.

Enough value gives the customer permission to say yes.

Never use slang or industry jargon. Only creates separation in communication. You need customers comfortable. Not confused or uncertain as to your meaning of strange new words they have never heard before.

When setting appointments always give them a choice. Is Wed. afternoon or Thurs. evening more convenient for you?

Picking a quarter hour creates the impression that you are busy and precise.

The only thing to sell over the phone is an appointment to meet in person. Be quick and to the point.

Never ask a question that you do not already know the answer to. When possible, always answer a question with a question.

Why is that important to you? If we can include that desired feature, are you ready to act right now?

It is not enough just uncovering why they will buy. It is getting them to say and feel that new solution out loud.

Hearing their own words from their mouth is much more persuasive than anything you can ever say.

The sales profession is a people business. Talk to as many potential buyers as possible. Don't get caught up in busy work and preparation. Concentrate on money making activities.

The more people you ask to buy. The more sales you will make. Ask every customer to buy multiple times.

Believe in your product or service. Without your complete personal conviction, you cannot transfer the necessary excitement and energy to others.

"No" is never a final answer. It just means they need additional information and more stimulated emotion.

Never give a price reduction during negotiations without some plausible justification. People will always be suspicious that they are paying too much.

Always ask for some reciprocal concession from the buyer. If I can get that done for you, will you do this for me?

Get referrals, letter of recommendation, etc. to balance the negotiations.

Paint vivid word pictures of the client already owning your product. Let them see and feel their personal ownership benefits.

Tell me how and where you are going to use it first. Go into great detail.

Change voice inflection to raise excitement. Keep customer engaged.

Great technique to keep young children quiet is asking them to draw you a picture. Have crayons and scratch paper close by in the closing area.

People must emotionally feel and speak why they want to buy right now, or they never will.

Can't say it enough times. **Emotion, not logic is trigger for immediate action**.

You only get objections by asking questions. You need them to determine how much the customer is engaged.

Just teaching and telling leads to a monologue with no selling.

Continually ask for more clarification. **What do you mean? Please tell me more. How does that make you feel? Why is that important to you?**

Sell fun and dreams with vivid mental images of them already owning and using your product.

Don't just deliver a product education. Paint wonderful ownership pictures with the customer and family right in the middle of them.

Encourage them to share those personal visions with you.

Always stretch the customer's comfort zone out as far as possible. Risk being disliked.

Have the mindset of always taking the customer one step further in the sales process than they want to go.

Patience and firm resolve are essential when closing. At some point in the sales process every negotiation will get more intense.

Stay strong and don't talk too much. **Silence is much more powerful after asking them to buy**.

The human brain can only receive and absorb three tiny bits of information at one time.

KISS. Keep it simple stupid. Resist flooding them with too much information.

Number your points as you make them.

Stop often to recap what has just been said. Don't risk mental overload or meltdown by introducing too much all at once.

A few key benefits that are important to them are much more effective than a long laundry list of features they don't even care about.

Chapter 13 **STORIES THAT SELL**

Nobody likes to be told what to do. Especially be told to act right now. A good story helps them to figure it out for themselves.

- The more compelling and emotional you can paint your "stories that sell", the more money you will make in the sales profession.
- Stories deliver a powerful and reinforcing direction to the customer's behavior.
- Every story delivers a positive message and promotes a realization from within of what needs to be done right now.
- No personal stories about you, your family, or friends. They sound contrived.
- Use third party stories about people the customer can "see" and identify with.
- Customers that were in a similar situation that took positive action and have been successful at improving their lives.
- Often every story begins with: "You remind me of..."
- Use full names, dates, vivid descriptions, and detail to make the stories more real.
- A poignant story takes the customer to a mental third level place in their own lives.

- That special zone where they can feel benefits and taste success happening. Not thinking about spending money.
- A place where change and immediate action are possible.
- A new and better tomorrow is now within grasp today.
- **Sales stories don't tell them to buy. They encourage the customer to act for themselves.**

- People prefer hearing a meaningful story rather than being taught a lesson or told what to do.

- Help them relate to others experiencing a similar situation and how they successfully got through it.

Four rules of 3rd party stories.

- Must be **specific** by using great detail. Allow listeners to create sharper mental images of how success is also possible for them.

- **Relevant**. Similar situation relating to their current buying experience and concerns.

- Serve a **purpose**. Reinforce dominant buying motive, solve their problem or overcome an objection.

- Be true and **believable**.

- Stories that sell take a skeptical, fearful, or defensive customer away from logic and over into emotional agreement.

- With a good story they are not alone while in a very personal and stressful situation.

- Others have been there before and have achieved success.

- Great stories personalize the entire sales process.

- They encourage specific action and humanize benefits that others have already received.

- Unique ownership visions come from identifying with others success. Other people have done it before. They can too right now.

Sample Stories That Sell

The Catapult Story (importance of family)

You remind me of Mary Spurlock. She is a recent widow. She also has three kids about the same ages as yours. John Junior is now 11. Twin sisters Hannah and Sharon are both 6. Their father John Sr. was an anesthesiologist. They lived in Houston, Texas. The doctor had just recently died of cancer when I met the family.

Mary told me that coming to San Diego was their first vacation since the funeral. She confessed that she couldn't even remember the last extended vacation taken with the entire family. Seems her husband was a general partner in some medical group and worked over 80 hours per week. They hardly ever saw him because he worked so much.

While Mary and I were talking the two girls were quietly sitting on the floor playing with coloring books. Little John Jr. sat very close to his mother and was just listening. I was amazed at how well behaved he was. I asked him about school and what kind of sports he liked. He seemed very shy and did not say much. But when I asked him to tell me about his last vacation his entire face lit up.

He said it was two summers ago in Branson, Missouri. It was there that his dad had taught him how to do a back flip into the swimming pool. His whole face was glowing and even his sisters stopped what they were doing to listen. He described the pool, the weather that day and even the red cushions on the pool chairs. It was amazing just how vivid and detailed his descriptions were. Especially given that he was only nine years old at the time.

I didn't interrupt but was a little confused because I had also been to that same resort several times. I knew there were six huge pools but none of them had a diving board. I asked little John Jr. to describe just how his daddy had taught him to do that flip. What he said next was simply amazing.

It seems that Dr. Spurlock had invented this game he called catapult. He would have little John stand on the side of the pool with his back to the water. The doctor would then clasp his hands together. Have his son put one of his feet into the cupped hands while holding on to his dad's broad shoulders for support. The doctor would then rock up and down a few times. Then with a huge grunt he would hurl little Johnny up into the air while flipping the tiny feet over his head backwards.

It was a back flip from the side of the pool. I had never seen anyone doing that before and I have been to many public swimming pools. It was a great idea.

As John Jr. was describing this wonderful memory, I could see Mary beginning to shake and cry. Tears were welling up in my eyes as well. Little Johnny had no idea how powerful his story really was. It took some time for Mary and I to regroup and compose ourselves. How such a young child could remember such a precious lasting memory of his father was amazing.

Even though the kids had now been taken out of private school and the big house recently sold. And most certainly the family economic condition was far worse than it had been before. Mary bought that day right then and there. I did not have to convince her of just how important her family was. Or how precious every moment spent together can be. You just never know what the future will bring.

This story can be used for selling anything. You must transfer the emotional and visual images into the customer's brain. They must see and even feel the doctor's hands cupping together. See the young son being flung into the air head over heels. Hear the splash of the water as he lands safely into the pool.

Feel the impact of the son never forgetting those precious moments spent with his father. If the customer can connect with your story, it will pull out their own private third level emotions and memories. It will allow them to open up and share more of themselves with you.

Corvette Story (procrastination)

You remind me of a story that I just read in Car and Driver Magazine recently. The article even had pictures of an old weather-beaten barn and very dusty car cover. Unless it was a really elaborate hoax, this is one of the best stories I have ever read. Just imagine that it was you instead of the grain and livestock salesman driving through the Midwest that day.

He had stopped at a farm in Iowa to get driving directions. He noticed a small red for sale sign nailed to a fading old wooden fence. It was posted in front of a small white house. The sign simply read "car for sale". He went up to the house and met the little old woman that owned the farm. As he was getting directions he casually asked how much for the car? She said five hundred dollars. Curious, he asked to see it. Together they walked out to the barn where he pulled off an old, dirty, and very weathered tarp.

There sat a dusty but pristine bright cherry red 1968 Corvette convertible. It had chrome side headers, four speed manual transmission and a 427 cubic inch V-8 engine. He looked inside the immaculate interior and noticed that the odometer only had 180 miles on it.

It seems the woman's son Jacob had bought the car and drove it back from the dealership to the farm. Soon thereafter he went off to fight in the Vietnam War. He did not come home, and his body was never recovered. She had kept that car in her barn for over 40 years waiting for her son to return. At this time her husband Jack had just recently passed away. Now she was old, tired and finally gave up hope of her son ever returning home.

The grain salesman asked her the price again. It was not fifty thousand dollars. Not even five thousand. She only wanted five hundred dollars. She certainly knew that the car was worth much more than what she was asking. But she didn't care. Money was not her concern. She said it would be nice for someone to finally get to drive the car. She knew her son would want that. She didn't want profit. She just wanted to let go. Her husband was now gone now and her son not coming home. It was time for her to move on.

Would you have bought that car? Would you have had to go home and think about it? Or check with your brother-in-law or attorney? Of course not! That is what recognizing value is all about. When you see an opportunity that improves your life there is no reason not to act immediately. It is simply making an informed decision to move forward. That is what you can do here today. This is your Corvette moment.

The happy ending to this story was that the guy did buy the car. He paid her ten thousand dollars and was happy to do it.

Wedding Story (commitment)

What is your anniversary date? Do you remember exactly what time of day the two of you got married? (10AM) So at 9AM you were both single? And at 11AM the two of you were married. Is that right? What exactly happened in that short period of time that changed your status together forever? It is not exchanging rings, vows or getting a license. It is none of that. It is making a lifelong commitment to each other. Having the courage to act and know deep down in your heart and soul it is the right thing for both of you to do. That is what I am encouraging you to do here again today. Make another commitment to yourselves. Do this today for a better life. Take another positive step forward together. Does that make sense to you?

CONCLUSION

- Have a set presentation. Know where you are going. Cover all 7 steps to the sale. Never skip or omit any of them.

- Find emotion and stir it up. **PAIN** or **GAIN** is always where to look. Question upon question to uncover and ignite their passion.

- People buy things from a third level mental state. Excitement not intellect is where you need to take them

- Listen more than you talk. When you do speak it should only be to encourage them to become more engaged. Find any topic that interests them and stay with it.

- You need to promote dialogue. Uncover valuable personal information from them. You don't get that when you are talking.

- A features and benefits monologue will never reveal why they will buy.

- Why? How does that make you feel? Please tell me more. Use these types of questions as tools to build their desire and passion.

- **PAIN** or **GAIN** are always the two primary motivating factors for any purchase. Hopefully both elements are powerfully present.

- Which one is pulling strongest upon them at this very moment?

- Frustration, bitterness, or anger with any specific current situation they are now facing. Or perhaps some powerful feelings arise while describing some traumatic experience buried way back in the past?

- Help them to be excited, jubilant, and extremely receptive to all new future possibilities. Timing is perfect to step forward to newer and better things in their lives.

- Both scenarios are just as persuasive and must be found through questioning.

- Everything you say and do should be about them and their current emotional state.

- A stimulated mind is where people buy from. Once they do become emotionally engaged; tie your product or service to that energy.

- To be successful in the selling profession you must ask good enough questions to get the potential customer involved.

- You accomplish this by being sensitive, compassionate, and truly listening to every word they speak. Only then can you process what they are saying.

- Watching their eyes, bodies, and mannerisms as they share their story with you will reveal even more clues as to what path to take the conversation down.

- Know in the back of your mind that before you can sell anything they must tell you what they want and why they want it.

- It certainly sounds much easier than it is in real life. Even if you just sell one single product the questioning is the same.

- Never just assume that the customer wants to buy only what you have to sell. Ask them and let them speak.

- Help them to clarify their passion and desire. Let them hear their own words, not yours. Help them to share their story with you.

- Final, final bit of advice for selling anything. **It is ALWAYS emotion and not analytics that closes a sale.**

- No matter how uninformed, educated or sophisticated the potential customer is. Or how complicated the product or service might be.

- Or the dollar amounts involved in the transaction. You as the salesperson must inject emotion into the situation.

- Wake the potential client up emotionally with great questioning. Always look for their unique **PAIN** or **GAIN** motivation.

- It is the stimulated emotional state that allows them to pull the trigger and say yes!

For those who desire any further elaboration about any points described in this book. They can be found in the book SELLING SKILLS by BW GATES available on Amazon.com and Kindle.

www.ingramcontent.com/pod-product-compliance
Lightning Source LLC
Chambersburg PA
CBHW070811220526
45466CB00002B/631